NEVER MIND THE
BLU^{THE}_{E}BIRDS

NEVER MIND
BLU^{THE}EBIRDS

The Ultimate
CARDIFF
CITY
QUIZ BOOK

DAVID COLLINS
& GARETH BENNETT

Foreword by DAVID GILES

The
History
Press

*Dedicated to anyone who has ever driven to
Mansfield on a wet Tuesday night, watched
Cardiff City lose 1–0, then had a puncture on the
way home . . . this book is for you.*

First published 2012

The History Press
The Mill, Brimscombe Port
Stroud, Gloucestershire, GL5 2QG
www.thehistorypress.co.uk

British Library Cataloguing in Publication Data.
A catalogue record for this book is available from the British Library.

ISBN 978 0 7524 7970 5

Typesetting and origination by The History Press
Printed in Great Britain

Contents

Foreword

By David Giles

(Cardiff City 1974–8 and 1985–7)

Are you like me when stood at the bar, chatting around the water cooler or kicking a ball around the playground? Do you test your mates with the latest football trivia . . . who was the biggest . . . who was the first . . . who was the last?

Well, if so and if, like me, you are a Bluebird through and through, then this is the book for you. David and Gareth have put together the ultimate Cardiff City quiz book. It's packed with teasers about players, goals, grounds – the lot. There are questions on songs, kits, obscure players I have never heard of and guys I played with myself.

I hope you have fun grappling with the questions. I was stumped more than once myself . . . though I know there is one I definitely have right!

Introduction

Be honest, we have all been there. We jump in the car for the long away trip, it's up north – it's always up north. Someone is late because he has a hangover but we eventually manage the entire pick-up and it's excited chatter all the way to Monmouth (maybe even as far as Ross-on-Wye in a good season). Then everyone has their head in the papers.

The driver is staring into space, the navigator is reading last week's programme, the back seat has unfolded the broadsheets, sweets are being sucked.

'I see Plymouth are away at Walsall today,' pipes a voice from the back.

Everyone momentarily gazes out of the window, hoping to spy a convoy of Argyle coaches and vans full of the 'Green Aaaaarmy' but . . . nothing.

'What's Walsall's ground called these days then?' asks the driver, 'is it still the Bescot Stadium?'

In a trice, the boredom is gone – the great away-trip-quiz is up and running. As we head north, people are posing questions about Walsall's nickname (the Saddlers), West Bromwich Albion's home ground (The Hawthorns) or the name of Stoke's old stadium (the Victoria Ground). A trip to Preston can pass in the blink of an eye under such circumstances.

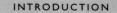

If you recognise these events . . . this is the book for you.

If you have forked out your hard-earned cash, then it is money well spent. If it's a present from the girlfriend then she wants commitment. If Santa has delivered it to you then clearly, you have been good (for goodness sake!). Open the book – it doesn't matter if you are in the pub, the playground or the retirement home for the terminally bewildered. There are questions for everyone; there are corny, cryptic teasers; there are mind-boggling questions to invoke silence among the keenest of City diehards. Some rounds are fun, some are straightforward, some are just annoying!

There are eleven questions in each round, just as there are eleven players in a Cardiff City team. Not all the questions are brilliant of course – but maybe not all of the players are either! There are easy questions, there are hard ones, there is one which NO-ONE will get right!

See – Preston isn't that far is it?

Enjoy the book.

David Collins & Gareth Bennett

(and yeah, we know, Walsall play at the Banks's Stadium!)

How This Book Works

This is a quiz book. We ask the questions and you shout out the answers. Write them down if you want, we don't mind. The book is as up-to-date as a quiz book ever could be but inevitably, some answers might change over the years. We may move to a new stadium again, sack the manager, or win the Champions League the day after you buy this book. Anything could happen. So we have had to introduce a cut-off point – think of it as closing the transfer window. All answers are therefore believed to be correct at September 2012. So if, say, we have signed Wayne Rooney after this date, THAT is why he does not feature in any questions we have drafted. It's because it hasn't happened yet.

Also, we have constructed the questions and answers ourselves. As far as we are aware, every answer is correct. Where there is doubt, we have checked the information against other, reliable sources. We have consulted reference books, waded through press cuttings and scrapbooks and asked some blokes up the pub. But the answers are ours and if any are wrong, then we will hold up our hands and admit the error.

But if you think that it wasn't Adrian Alston who scored against Bury in 1976 because from where you were stood it looked like it hit Tony Evans on the way in, hard cheese. The quizmaster is always right!

Round

1

The 'Current Affairs' Round

Welcome to our book. We hope you enjoy this meander through the history of our football club, turning stones along the way, with trips and stumbles over how much you really know about Cardiff City Football Club. We start with a straightforward round, all about our recent fortunes. Get stuck into these. But a word of warning, like all things Cardiff City, it gets harder as you go on. Come on City!

1 Who missed a penalty for the Bluebirds against Crystal Palace in the Carling Cup in 2012?

2 Talking of Palace, what was Darcy Blake's squad number for City during 2011/12?

3 Which team knocked Cardiff City out of the FA Cup during 2012?

4 . . . and who knocked us out of the Capital One Cup in 2012?

5 Who scored our first league goal of the 2012/13 season?

6 Which former City star both scored and missed a penalty for Team GB in the 2012 Olympics? (in the same match!)

7 Okay, no more putting it off. The rebranding. Which two current Cardiff City players are depicted on the external fascia of the 'rebranded' Cardiff City Stadium?

8 Which 85-year-old ex-City manager passed away in September 2012?

9 He turned it down, but Ben Turner is eligible to play for Wales. How does he qualify?

10 He scored his first goal for City away to Millwall, but from which club did we sign Craig Noone?

11 Finally, relive the agony. Can you name the five City penalty takers from the 2012 Carling Cup final?

Round 2

Singing the Blues

Are you a diehard over many years of suffering like us? Through the years, have the antics of the City supporters often provided more entertainment than the players themselves? If so, then this musical round is the round for you. Can you identify the City stars from these chants?

> 'Sing when you're Quizzing!
> You only sing when you're Quizzing!'

No extra prizes for singing along, mind.

1   Early wearer of the Magic Hat. Joined Norwich in 2005. Did he really fancy that?
2   He got the ball and scored a goal. 22 goals in the Third Division during the 1982/83 season if truth be told.
3   Iconic City legend immortalised in melodic allegations around gaming machine irregularities.
4   Who needs Cantona, when we've got Stantona?
5   'Open the Score Richards.' A real goal-den oldie this one.

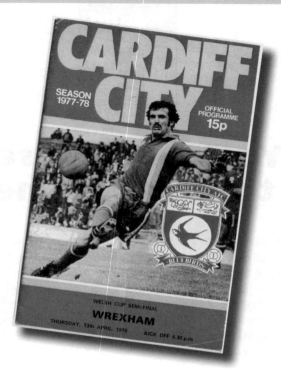

6   31 goals in 75/76. He could walk on water this lad!

7   Took Joe Ledley's advice and didn't sign for Celtic in 2010.
    Remix of question 1. Ah well, if the hat fits . . .

8   Ah, the love of my life. I want silver hair too!

9   What's that coming over the hill? An automatic entry in
    any City hit parade.

10 He had no hair. We didn't care.

11 Psycho! Psycho! More of a chant than a song. But who
    was 'Psycho' back in the '90s?

You're Supposed to Be at Home!

Ah, we have all heard the stories of how Ninian Park was a hotbed of passion, a hostile arena to send fear into the hearts of men. But how much do you remember about our much-loved former home? Did you ever gaze around the stadium while munching on your half-time pasty, wondering about the history of those ancient surroundings? Do you recall the tall, elastic floodlights pointing their steely fingers to the sky; the enormous Bob Bank; the mighty Grange End – dark and cavernous – the long wooden seats of the old Canton Stand? If you have turned misty-eyed and nostalgic in recalling any of these images, then this is the round for you. Come on baby, let the good times roll . . .

1   When did the club move to Ninian Park?

2   Who was the ground named after?

3   Who were our first opponents there?

4   For how many years did the Captain Morgan's Rum advert 'grace' the roof of the Bob Bank?

5 When was the roof taken off the Grange End? And when was it put back on?

6 When did the 'new' Grandstand – spanning the length of the pitch – first open?

7 When was the first Rugby League game played at Ninian Park?

8 Which boxing world championship bout was fought there in the late 1960s?

9 Which legendary musical performer played there in 1976?

10 And which other renowned international 'superstar' appeared there as part of his 1982 British Tour?

11 What was Phil Suarez's role at Ninian Park?

One-Hit Wonders

Each answer is a simple one-word answer. But just to spice it up a little, the last letter of each answer is the first letter of the next. You'll get the hang of it . . .

1   Legendary City full-back from the 1960s. Was hit by a bottle thrown in the away leg with Real Madrid in 1971. Gary . . . ?

2   Mighty Reds who paid £110,000 for our star striker in 1971. Carling Cup foes years later.

3   Dutch defender. Had a goal disallowed at Wembley in 2008. Glenn . . .

4   Legendary 1960s City boss. See you Jimmy!

5   Back where it all started – in 1899.

6   Record-breaking City hero. His mum calls him Robert, but to us he'll always be . . .

7 Amazing 1980s Swap Shop saw Jones, Micallef and Lewis head to Newport in exchange for Vaughan and . . .

8 Famous Scot – actually from the Valleys though. Legendary FA Cup strike against Leeds.

9 Infamous home end takes it name from this Cardiff district.

10 Ex-City manager – hundreds of appearances for answer no 2. Phil . . .

11 'Lethal' 1980s midfielder. Ex-Baggie. Steve . . .

12 (Thank goodness there is not a twelfth man in this round!)

Round

5

Early Days

Right then, enough of all this cryptic frivolity. This is supposed to be a proper quiz book after all, so let's have a few grown-up rounds. Start at the very beginning as Julie Andrews would say (we happen to know that Julie rarely misses a home game). We are guessing that not too many of you would have been around back in 1899 when it all began, but this round will appeal to the historians among you. The questions loosely cover the period up to the outbreak of the Second World War, but stick with it – you'll be surprised at how many of these you know, you know.

1   Who was the founder of the football club?

2   What was the club's original name?

3   What were the original colours?

4   Where did they originally play their home games?

5   And when did they become Cardiff City?

6   Who became Cardiff City's first ever professional player in June 1910? He was born in Bala and played for the club until 1926. He won 8 Welsh caps and was signed by the answer to question 1 . . . as if that helps.

7   On their march to Wembley in 1927, Cardiff City adopted a small cat as their mascot. The cat was a regular sight at City games and died in 1939. We know, you can see this coming, but . . . what was the name of the cat?

8   Who was City's manager throughout the 1920s?

9   What tragic event occurred in January 1930?

10   And what other misfortune occurred in January 1937?

11   Who were City league runners-up to in 1924? By how many points did they lose the league title?

Round 6

Bluebirds Bad Boys

Let's be honest, over the years we have had our share of (ahem) 'characters' eh? How many of these loveable rogues stick in your mind?

1   The Greatest Footballer You Never Saw?

2   Temperamental Geordie. Well-publicised car park bust-up with coach Alan Sealey back in 1978.

3   Volatile Trowbridge tearaway. Ex-Celtic, Coventry, West Ham. Liked a round of golf too perhaps?

4   Another Geordie. Enjoyed a flutter we hear. Later betting on Tractor Races maybe?

5   Never shy in speaking his mind – just ask Bobby Gould! Now a media darling.

6   The youngest player ever to be sent off for Cardiff City.

7   Fleet-footed youngster nabbed from QPR. Off the field issues never far from the surface unfortunately. Just a few weeks after joining the Bluebirds he tested positive

for class A drugs and was handed a two-year suspended sentence by the Football Association of Wales. Moved on in 2002.

8 This local hero faced up to his demons by coming clean over the booze. Scored twice against Cardiff City for our West Country cousins Bristol City during 2002/03.

9 Sent off twice against the Swans. That's taking a Liberty that is.

10 Never-to-be-forgotten exchange with Luton's Milija Aleksic.

11 Amazing record of antics for our last Bad Boy. Incidents with Belgian police during Euro 2000, jailed following our famous FA Cup win over Leeds United and banned from football grounds for six years. Worse still though, he used to play for Swansea City! But can you tell us who he is?

Pride of Wales!

Well why not? Who can forget those magnificent Welsh Cup triumphs over Sully and Cardiff Corries, Arms Park glory against northern giants Wrexham and Rhyl, and cut-and-thrust cup clashes against Toshack's Swans (oops, we lost that one didn't we . . .)? Amazingly perhaps, the Welsh Cup has thrown up moments of real drama over the years, and, as we shall see later, set us up for some of the most famous nights in the club's history. But how much do you recall about these epic battles of the Principality?

1 How many times have City won the Welsh Cup?
2 And where do they rank on the all-time list of winners?
3 Where did we beat Wrexham 2–0 in the 1988 final? And who scored City's second goal in that game, following a 'mazy dribble?' Ironic really . . .
4 Time to step back a few years now. City trainer George Latham 'did a Les Sealey' when the Blues lifted the Welsh Cup for the first time in 1912. What happened exactly?
5 When City won the FA Cup in 1927, how far did they get in the Welsh Cup?
6 When was the first final involving City at the National Stadium?
7 Which English teams did City beat in the finals of 1968, 1974 and 1992? And where the hell is that last place?
8 Why were City's Steve Mokone and Swansea's Harry Griffiths sent off during a 1960 'Battle of the Vetch'?
9 Why was City's 1992 quarter-final away to Swansea postponed?
10 Who scored City's last ever goal in the Welsh Cup, in the 1995 final?
11 And where was that last match played?

Stars in OUR Eyes

One of the joys of a book like this, apart from its ability to while away a long car journey, is that we get to indulge ourselves. Skipping through the pages, well, it's like having your own Bluebirds time machine isn't it? From the flickering black-and-white images of 1927 glory, through to the full-colour 24-hour surround-sound era that is football in the new millennium. So many well-remembered faces from days of yore. Most of the book sets out to test your knowledge of established City legends – the Nathan Blakes, Robert Earnshaws, the Toshacks and Clarks. Of course these guys are all – to a greater or lesser extent – fellas that have shot to fame having had little or no previous claim to glory.

It hasn't always been that way of course. From time to time – especially in recent years – City have snapped up the odd proper 'legend' – a star in the twilight years of their glory, sometimes coming 'home' for one last lap of honour.

They haven't all worked out of course. For every Craig Bellamy there's been a Russell Osman. For every legend-in-his-own-lifetime, there's been a legend-in-his-own-opinion. But make no mistake. We have had our share of big names over the years. Proper players that you've seen on telly and everything. See what you can remember about these guys . . .

Robbie Fowler (2007/08)

1   From which club did former Anfield hero Robbie Fowler join Cardiff City?

2   Against which club did Robbie score 2 goals for City in a Carling Cup tie?

3   How many Premier League titles has Robbie won?

4   With which other former Liverpool legend did Robbie Fowler invest in a number of racehorses?

5   What was the nickname given to Robbie by the Anfield fans?

John Charles (1963–6)

1 In which UK city would you find 'John Charles Way'?
2 For which club did John Charles appear against Cardiff City in the 1968 Welsh Cup final?
3 How many Welsh caps did Big John win?
4 The 'Gentle Giant' played for Juventus and which other Italian club?
5 John Charles is part of a famous football family. Can you name his nephew who won 19 caps for Wales between 1980 and 1986?

Gerry Francis (1984)

1   How many England caps did ex QPR skipper Gerry
    Francis win . . . ?
2   . . . and how many of those came as captain?
3   To what league position did Francis lead QPR in 1976?
4   In later years, Gerry Francis went on to manage Spurs
    and QPR, but how many appearances did he make for us
    in the 1980s?
5   How many goals did he score for us?

Craig Bellamy (2010/11 and 2012–)

1   Which manager wrote about Craig, 'He was a great
    player wrapped round an unusual and volatile character'?
2   What award did Craig receive at the end of the 2002
    season?
3   In which West African country has Craig set up a Football
    Foundation?
4   With which club did Craig first turn professional and
    make his league debut?
5   We all remember that Craig scored that famous
    Bellissimo goal against Italy in 2002, but who was the
    goalie he rounded to score that night?

Kevin Ratcliffe (1993)

1 Against which northern club did Kevin Ratcliffe score his only goal for Cardiff City (on his debut, no less)?

2 And against which country did he win his only international cap as a Cardiff City player?

3 Who were Everton's FA Cup final opponents when Rats skippered the Toffees to victory in 1984?

4 Which record-breaking Welsh keeper kept goal for Everton that day?

5 Which two clubs did Kevin Ratcliffe once manage?

ADMIT TO GROUND

(Enter at Turf End Turnstiles 17, 18, 19,
20, 21, 22, 23 or 24)

№ 2143

British International
Championship

WALES v. **ENGLAND**
Racecourse Ground, Wrexham
SATURDAY, 17th MAY, 1980

Kick-off 3.00 p.m.

Admission £1.50

Secretary,
The F.A. of Wales.

Mike England's finest hour?

Mike England (1975/76)

1   What is Mike England's first name?

2   Which club was he with prior to joining Spurs in 1966?

3   At which ground did Mike England score his only Cardiff
City goal?

4   How many of his 44 caps for Wales did Mike England gain
as a Cardiff City player?

5   Which US team did he join upon leaving Cardiff City in
1976?

The Road to Wembley

Ah, now you're talking. As youngsters we used to love the FA Cup final – what the players wore, meet the wives, cup final *It's a Knockout* . . . but that was all simply the stuff of dreams, the days of coats for goalposts and three-and-in. We'd never get to Wembley in real life would we . . . *would* we?

1 A nice easy one to start. How many times have City actually won the FA Cup?

2 And how many times have they reached the final?

3 A bit trickier now. How many times have Cardiff City played an FA Cup tie at Wembley?

4 Giant-killers now – who scored the winning goals for the Bluebirds against Leeds in 2002, Manchester City in 1994 and Spurs in 1977?

5 In which four seasons did City reach (at least) the semi-final stage of the FA Cup?

6 During our FA Cup run in 2008, what was historic about our third round tie at Chasetown? And where exactly is Chasetown?

7 A tricky one, this. In 1946, City were drawn at home to West Bromwich Albion in the third round. After a 0–0 draw at Ninian, City lost 4–0 at The Hawthorns to go out of the competition. However, this second game was not a replay – what was it, then?

8 Who scored the goals in our 2–0 win over Middlesbrough at the Riverside Stadium to send us to Wembley in 2008?

9 And who scored the goals in our 2–1 win at Ayresome Park – Boro's former ground – back in 1994?

10 Remarkably, against which non-league team were City drawn to play away three times between 1988 and 1994?

11 City were also drawn away in an unlikely Welsh derby game in 1987. Who were their opponents?

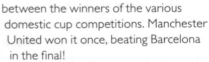

Round 10

Jeux Sans Frontières

If you are below a certain age, you may find it hard to believe that Cardiff City were once a genuine force on the European stage. All right, 'force' may be stretching the point perhaps, but back in the days before Sky TV invented the Champions League, Cardiff City were regular competitors in something called the European Cup Winners' Cup. We kid ye not, this was a proper competition played on a home-and-away basis round-by-round between the winners of the various domestic cup competitions. Manchester United won it once, beating Barcelona in the final!

As regular winners of the Welsh Cup, Cardiff City enjoyed a frequent passport to travels around the Continent, rubbing shoulders with the mighty . . . and the unheard-of. These days it's all been absorbed into the Europa League of course, with the Welsh Cup winners crossing swords with teams from

34

Finland and Moldova sometime around early June. Channel 5 has replaced the glory-glory nights on a Thursday. Back then though, these were memorable evenings at Ninian Park.

Or were they? Let's see how much sticks in your mind from this era.

1 In what year did City play their first European Cup Winners' Cup tie, and who were the opponents?

2 How far did City get in that first campaign? Who eventually knocked us out?

3 In the 14 years between 1964 and 1978, how many seasons did City not play in Europe?

4 What was our best ever run – which year, and how far did we get?

5 In the Moscow Torpedo tie that year, where did we play the away leg? And for an extra point, which country is that city now in?

6 Where did we play the replay? Give yourself an extra point if you went!

7 Which two teams did we beat in 1971 to set up the quarter-final tie against Real Madrid?

8 Who scored a hat-trick to put us through against Derry City in 1989, and what was unusual about Derry's position in the competition?

9 What did Madness have to do with City's run that year?

10 Who was our last European tie against, in the 1994 season? And who scored City's three goals in that tie?

11 Finally – who threw the bottle at Gary Bell in that away leg in Madrid in 1971? Nah, only kidding. What was the score in that match, though?

Round 11

Connect Four

Enough of all this serious stuff then, this next round is more of a game than a quiz. But it's a tricky one . . . with a sting in the tail (or should that be tale?). Can you spot the connections between the answers in each round?

Connect I

1 Captain of Wales against Norway in 2011.

2 Brother of the Gentle Giant. Joined City in 1962 from – well, that would be telling.

3 Name our Scottish bird-watching former goalkeeper.

4 One of Dave Jones' many loan signings – scored a cracker against Hull City. Later joined Ipswich Town to line up alongside Chopra.

So . . . what's the connection between these answers?

Connect 2

Are you getting the hang of it? Let's move on. Maybe a trickier bunch here…

1   Ex-Watford striker who starred for City and Swansea.
2   Two spells as City boss. 1969 League Cup winner.
3   2004 loan signing, who later starred for Middlesbrough. Captained England at under-21 level.
4   Former Orient defender signed for us in 1976. Played a few games up front too. He came, he saw, he went!

And again . . . spot the link between these answers.

Connect 3

All of the answers in this round are Welshmen. But that's not the answer we're looking for.

1   North Walian defender who later joined South Wales Police. Think early 1970s.
2   Joined City at the same time as the answer above! Alan Warboys headed the other way as part of the deal.
3   Goalkeeper, sadly no longer with us following premature passing in 1993.
4   Starred for Bolton, Wolves and Blackburn. 11 goals for us in 1992/93.

. . . And the connection is?

Connect 4

Have we saved the toughest until last? Read on . . .

1   Another ex-City and ex-Swan. Palace too. Goalscorer
    in famous 1980 Wales triumph against England at
    The Racecourse. Media pundit.
2   Home town of the Beast!
3   This guy's former clubs include Cardiff City, Wrexham
    and Baltimore Blasts! Diminutive midfielder who joined
    us in 1979. Left us after a few discontent winters.
4   Top scorer at Ninian Park with 18 goals in 1983/84.
    An impressive total for a winger.

So, have you worked out the connection yet?

Connect the Connections!

Finally, what links all four of these connections?

A Cup by Any Other Name . . .

Well we had to didn't we? After our heroics in 2011/12, the League Cup has enjoyed a higher profile than ever before among City diehards. Who'd have thought it, eh? The Football League Cup, introduced in 1960, has also been known as the Milk Cup (1982–6), the Littlewoods Cup (1986–90), the Rumbelows Cup (1990–2), the Coca-Cola Cup (1992–8), the Worthington Cup (1998–2003), the Carling Cup (2003–12) and now the Capital One Cup.

But for our purposes, it's just the 'League Cup', okay? A cup by any other name would smell as sweet.

1   Prior to 2011/12, what was City's best performance in the League Cup? Who eventually knocked us out?
2   City's left-back for the home leg of the above tie was the brother of a future Wales manager. Who was he?
3   In the 1977 competition, who bagged all four goals at Eastville Stadium in a 4–4 thriller, which put us through (on aggregate) against Bristol Rovers?

4   Another obscure one here – much like those early rounds on long-forgotten Tuesday nights. Which future City player kept goal against us for Arsenal in our 1983 tie?

5   How did City get through the second round in 1987 without playing anyone . . . ?

6   . . . and which top-flight side did they beat in the third round?

7   Can you recall who was managing City for their first round second leg tie at Plymouth in August 1989, when City courageously responded to a 3–0 home defeat in the first leg by winning 3–1, and almost battled their way through? That was his only game in charge, by the way.

8   We also lost over two legs in the first round of the 1997
    tournament. What was significant about our opponents,
    in the context of that season?

9   In 2000 and 2001, we went out in ties where the away leg
    was played at the same ground – although we played two
    different opponents. Who were they?

10 Earnie's League Cup hat-trick came in a first round away
    tie in 2003 – a 5–1 win. Who were the opponents?
    Cheers if you get that one right!

11 Where did we lose in the 2008 tournament – the first
    time we had played there for 48 years?

Round

13

Dad or Chips?

Time for a breather now – time to give the old grey matter a rest. Or maybe not. We are sure you are all familiar with this game. You know the one. You are at a bar with your mates and set yourself fantasy quandaries where you get to choose between Kylie or Dannii, or Brad Pitt and Justin Timberlake. Or even just custard creams or Hob Nobs (ooh, that's a tough one . . .).

Anyway, there are no right answers, this round is all down to you. Simply state your preference. Just for fun though, we

have included our own choices in the answer pages. This kind of game used to feature in the programme by the way – 'Ant's Quickfire Ten', presumably drawn up by 'contributor' Anthony Redwood. Do you remember him? No, nor do we.

Oh, and by the way, the first one, we don't mean the Aussie soap, okay?

1   Home or Away?
2   Jones or Mackay?
3   Earnie or Chops?
4   Don Murray or Phil Dwyer?
5   Black away kit or yellow?
6   FA Cup glory or Premier League promotion?
7   City or Wales? (gulp!)
8   Behind the goal or on the side?
9   Ninian Park or the Cardiff City Stadium?
10 The Vetch Field or the Liberty?
11 Fanzines or the message boards?
12 Standing or sitting?
13 Jeff Hemmerman or Jimmy Gilligan?
14 Toshack or Clark?
15 'The Ayatollah' or 'Men of Harlech'?
16 Routledge or Burke?
17 Len Ashurst or Frank Burrows?
18 The Grange End or the Bob Bank?
19 Paul Parry or Glenn Loovens? (ooh err!)
20 Craig Bellamy or Ryan Giggs?

Round 14

Derby Delights

Ah the joys of our friendly rivalry. Friends or foes, like 'em or loathe 'em, you just can't escape the tension of the South Wales derbies. But how much do you recall about our clashes with the Swans? Just try these simple brainteasers, which are all simply 'True or False' answers. Off you go then . . .

1 Don Murray played for Swansea.
2 Phil Dwyer played for Swansea.
3 Leigh Barnard once scored after 1 minute 45 seconds at the Vetch.
4 Alan Curtis has scored for Swansea against Cardiff and for Cardiff against Swansea.
5 John Charles once scored an own goal while playing for Swansea against Cardiff City.
6 John Toshack managed both clubs.
7 Frank Burrows is the only man to have managed both clubs.

8   Brothers David Giles and Paul Giles each had spells at both clubs.

9   'Pitch invasion mars wartime clash.' (Have we made this up?)

10 Cardiff City have never kept a clean sheet at the Liberty Stadium.

11 In the famous 1980 clash at Ninian Park, which ended so dramatically thanks to a certain John Buchanan, Swansea wore all-white.

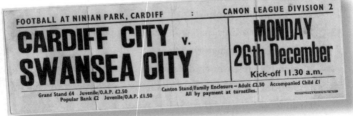

John Toshack scored in this game in 1983. He remarked that 'many things have changed at Ninian Park over the years, but at least the goals were still in the same place!'

Round 15

The Swinging Sixties

It is often said that, if you can remember the 1960s, you weren't really there. Well, maybe this is true if you hung out at Woodstock, the Cavern Club or Carnaby Street, but does it work in Sloper Road? Test yourself with this round of Beatlemania . . . sorry – 'Bluebirdmania'.

1   Who did City beat 1–0 at Ninian in April 1960, a top-of-the-table clash to secure promotion to the First Division?

2   What was the attendance at Ninian that day, and what was significant about it?

3   Which future City manager made 5 appearances in City's promotion campaign that year?

4   Which Mumbles-born defender's career was more or less ended by a Denis Law challenge in front of the Ninian Grandstand during the 1961 season?

5   City's final home game (to date!) in the top division of English football was against West Ham in April 1962. What was the attendance?

6   A famous Welsh international arrived at City in the
    summer of 1963. Who was he, and from whom did we
    sign him?

7   Who did Jimmy Scoular manage before his appointment
    by City?

8   City escaped relegation from the Second Division in the
    1966 season by beating Middlesbrough 5–3 at Ninian
    Park, sending Boro' down instead. This match was
    known afterwards as the finest performance of City's
    inconsistent outside-right, and was 'named after him'.
    Who was he?

9   Who was the first player to come on as a substitute in
    a City league game, in August 1965? For a second point,
    who were the opponents at Ninian that day?

10 City had two major cup exploits during this decade: they
    were beaten in the semis of the 1966 Football League
    Cup, and in the same stage of the 1968 Cup Winners'
    Cup. Name their opponents on both occasions.

11 Les Lea, Brian Clark and goalie Fred Davies were all
    signed by City in December 1967/January 1968. From
    which clubs did they arrive?

Round

16

The Biggest and the Best

Back to basics now, and it's time to don those thinking caps again. This round is pretty straightforward. We all know our stuff on the Bluebirds record-breakers don't we – who scored the most, who cost the most, etc. Try your luck with these, then. No gimmicks in this round – just our best-ever XI questions. And, if you are clever, you might find the odd clue tucked away.

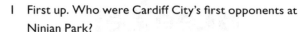

1 First up. Who were Cardiff City's first opponents at Ninian Park?

2 Who scored more goals in the Football League for Cardiff City – John Toshack or Brian Clark?

3 Who has played in goal most often for the Bluebirds?

4 Who has made the most European appearances for City?

5 How many league goals did Robert Earnshaw score for Cardiff City in 2002/03?

6 6 of the best – who is the only player to score 6 goals in a competitive match for Cardiff City?

7 Who has scored the most hat-tricks for Cardiff City? (Bonus point if you know how many.)

8 Who bagged 8 goals for Cardiff City in a friendly against Rhayader in 1980?

9 Who was the first player to cost Cardiff City £1million?

10 How many Welsh caps did Phil Dwyer win?

11 Who scored Cardiff City's first goal of the 2011/12 season?

Krek Spelin pLeeZe!

Hee hee . . . you are going to like this one. The concept of this round is quite simple – grab a paper and pen and see if you can solve these tricky tongue-twisters. We have gone back to the points system for a bit of fun, but you only get the point if you can correctly spell each player's name – first name and surname! Got it? It's harder than wot u fink!

1   Okay, an easy one to start with. City's silver-haired right-back – and you have to get the capital letters right.

2   Our Finnish goalkeeper who appeared in the 2008 FA Cup final, dropped the ball, and then went bald.

3 Tall centre-forward from Northern Ireland who broke his leg on his only league start for us – then went to Aberdeen in 2010.

4 Dutch centre-back who went to Celtic after our FA Cup final appearance.

5 Twice on-loan enigmatic winger or midfielder, North Walian of Greek Cypriot extraction. Brilliant in his first loan spell (2006), less impact in his second (2011).

6 Utility player signed from West Bromwich Albion, Darren Purse's best mate, retired due to persistent injuries in December 2009.

7 Right, they are gonna get harder now! Centre-half from Hungary who can't get in the team (he will probably have been released by the time you read this).

8 Very tall African midfielder who came on a season's loan from Hull in 2010.

9 Japanese on-loan midfielder who had a good 'motor' on him.

10 Second-string goalie, originally from Neath, who retired and became our goalkeeping coach. Joined from Huddersfield Town in 2002.

11 Error-prone Greek goalie who came to us on loan from Coventry in the second half of the 2009 season.

Round 18

McBluebirds

It's amazing how many famous Bluebirds have come down from north o' the border over the years. See how many tartan terrors you can spot from the list below. Here's a warning though, they get harder as they go on – much like some Scotsmen we have met.

1. Midfielder who signed from Watford in the summer of 2011.
2. Goalkeeper who had a furious altercation with Anthony Gerrard in a televised game at Forest in 2010.
3. Full-back who made his league debut for City in the first league game at the new stadium (a 4–0 victory over Scunthorpe).

City had more players in the Scottish squad
for this game than in the Welsh squad.

4 A tougher one here. A six-pointer, you might say. Name the three Scots City signed from Rangers during the Dave Jones era.

5 Diminutive-looking Highlander with dynamite in his boots. He was City's leading goalscorer (from midfield) in the 1978 and 1979 seasons.

6 Captained City to their famous victory over Real Madrid in 1971.

7 Another inspiring skipper, he captained City's 1960 promotion-winning team.

8 Scored the winner in the 1927 FA Cup final, although ultimately a tragic figure.

9 In a 1924 Home International match at Ninian Park between Wales and Scotland, City supplied both captains: Fred Keenor captained Wales, but who skippered the Scots?

10 Name the five Scots who have managed City.
    A point for each!

11 Finally . . . the penalty-shoot out! From which clubs did
    City sign the following?

> Kevin McNaughton
> John Buchanan
> Freddie Pethard
> Jim Eadie
> Alec Milne

. . . and with which Scottish club had Buchanan previously
been associated?

Anoraknophobia!

Of course, it's not always a glamorous life is it? For every
'I was there' night against Real Madrid or Hamburg; for every
memorable cup clash against, Leeds, Arsenal or Liverpool, there
are those, well, shall we say, less memorable encounters.
Try these for size.

**WARNING
DO NOT TACKLE THIS
ROUND IF YOU POSSESS A
FEAR OF OBSCURITY!**

Away games in the FAW Premier Cup –
we have suffered for our art!

1 When City played Arsenal at Ninian Park in the summer of 1975, for which trophy were they competing?

2 In 1979, which of these competitions did Cardiff City actually enter: the Anglo-Italian Cup, the Watney Cup, the Texaco Trophy or the Anglo-Scottish Cup? (Clue: it's only one of them . . . and one of us went to an AWAY game in this competition!)

3 And can you remember any of the teams City played during that momentous campaign?

4 City played one of their most mysterious matches ever in the summer of 1980, a pre-season friendly against Hamilton Academical. What was so odd about it?

5 Who did City play in the Charity Shield in October 1927? What was the score? The only Welsh team to win the Charity Shield!

6 Which First Division outfit did City entertain at Ninian Park at the end of the 1981 season (losing 2–1 to them)?

7   Who did we play in the testimonials for Phil Dwyer
    (November 1982), Ron Healey (November 1983), Harry
    Parsons (summer 1995) and Jason Perry (summer 1996)?
8   Who went on a 5-goal blast against Rushden & Diamonds
    during a 7–1 Ninian Park win in the LDV Vans Trophy?
9   And who scored our last ever (hopefully!) goal in this
    competition in 2003?
10 Which overseas countries did City visit on a 14-game
    tour in the summer of 1968?
11 Which future City manager broke his leg (thus ending
    his playing career) while 'guesting' for City in a wartime
    game?

Award yourself an extra point if you ever actually attended any
of these games, by the way. Three points if you went to an away
game.

Cum On Feel the Noize!

Ah, the 1970s – the days of flared pants, Glam Rock and *Sportsnight with Coleman*. All matches kicked off at 3.00 p.m. on a Saturday afternoon and we wore silk scarves tied to our wrists. Music came in shiny, black discs bought from a *real* shop and David Collins had a bright orange Chopper! Indeed, those were the days my friend . . .

But how much can you remember from these wonderful days? Do names like Alston, Evans and Friday deliver you misty-eyed back to your adolescence? Or are you only 21 and thinking, 'What are they going on about?'

We've well and truly pushed the '70s boat out in this round. Who remembers Sunday lunchtimes with *Jimmy Saville's Old Record Club*, eh? Classic listening. Jimmy would award a point for the song; and a point for the artist. We've nicked his act for the round. So try these for size, guys and gals:

1   Hit duo from the start of the 1970s – golden boys from a golden era. We'll give you a point for each striker, one sadly no longer with us.

2   Who was the midfield dynamo who joined the Bluebirds from Coventry in the summer of 1970?

3   Which former Manchester United manager became City boss in October 1973?

4   Another two-pointer now from the pre-Sky TV era. Which City player was reported dead on BBC's *Grandstand* programme in 1975? But what really happened?

5   City escaped the drop with 1–1 draws at Ninian Park
    towards the end of both the 1974 and 1977 seasons.
    There's a point for each of their relegation-threatened
    opponents you can name (both of whom went down)
    from those games.

6   For two more points, who scored the City goals in those
    games?

7   Ah, the days of sideburns and stubble. But can you name
    the legendary 'understudy to George Best' who joined
    City for £60,000 in February 1973? And from which club
    did we sign him?

8   'City Sign World Cup Star!' Pelé? Müller? Cruyff? Guess
    again. Which star of the 1974 World Cup finals came to
    Ninian in the summer of 1975? Again, from which club did
    we get him?

9   Which tiny Scottish manager steered City to promotion
    from the Third Division in 1976? Yes, Jim really did fix it!

10 This is one to test you – we'll make this a six-pointer!
    What was the attendance (to the nearest thousand) for
    the classic six-pointer against promotion rivals Hereford
    United at Ninian Park that year? And what had happened
    in the build-up to that game, to influence the size of the
    crowd?

11 Finally, one for the real anoraks (or should that be, the
    tank tops?). Anyway, we want you to name the four men
    who managed City during the decade. And if you are
    really in the groove, everyone remembers the number
    ones from the 1970s . . . but can you name their number
    twos (i.e. their assistant managers)?

Round

21

Now That's What I Call Seventies

We feel you are getting the hang of all this by now so we've cranked up the intensity for this round. Eleven real toughies to test you. Indulge us while we continue our obsession with the 1970s won't you – but hey, it's only rock 'n' roll, right?

1   We imagine you all got the duo that kicked off the last round, but can you name City's not-so-famed striking duo in the 1979 season, when the Bluebirds recovered to finish 9th – their highest league finish for eight years (and yes, we did see him score!).

2   Which diminutive Scouse midfield general joined Cardiff City from Notts County (for just half a season) in November 1973?

3   Who succeeded Graham Keenor as club secretary (serving from 1972 to 1985)?

4   Who was the City physio who performed a life-saving operation on the pitch at Gillingham in 1975? (Hope you got this right in the last round!)

5   City challenged for promotion to the top flight three years running in the period 1968–71. But in which positions did City actually finish at the end of those campaigns?

6   Where did City seal promotion with a 1–0 victory on the last day of the 1976 season?

7   What was the score when struggling City went away to Luton for a Second Division fixture in September 1978?

8   Who was City's goalkeeper that afternoon?

9   *Match of the Day* really meant something back in the 1970s, and two City players figured heavily on the show during this decade. One had the programme's 'Save of the Season' in 1972; the other scored a spectacular goal in 1977, which featured for several weeks on *MoTD*'s opening credits sequence. Who were these City stars?

10 More dips into the record collection. What was the name of the resident band at the 'Bluebirds Club' in the mid-1970s? And what was their connection to a certain City midfielder? Honest!

11 And finally – this will kill you off. What was the nickname of the following players:

Phil Dwyer

Derek Showers

Linden Jones

Rod Thomas

Ray Bishop

An extra point if you can come up with a credible explanation for each of these nicknames. It doesn't have to be true!

Four-Four-Two

It's time for more mental dexterity now. This round is based on the most famous football formation of them all. The questions are all on the theme of fours, fours and twos – well, what did you expect? A round on football tactics, eh? Coming soon . . . the *catenaccio* round, the *Christmas tree* round and the *lump-it-forward-to-our-big-lazy-striker* round . . .

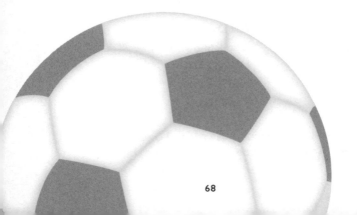

Four

1 Slick defender from City's days as a Euro force. Four caps
   for Wales. Think Davies, Carver, Bell, Sutton, Murray . . .

2 Which Scottish midfielder wore the black no. 4 shirt for
   the Bluebirds at Wembley in 2008?

3 Who is the only player to have played (and scored!) for
   four different Welsh clubs in the Football League?

4 Double the fun here, which City player wore number 44
   during his 2008–10 spell with the Bluebirds?

Four

5 Hat-trick hero in our 4–0 home win against Derry City
   in 1988.

6 This man scored 4 goals for City against Carlisle in 1971.

7 . . . and this one did it against Gillingham in 2003.

8 During the 1920s, who was our top scorer for four years
   on the trot?

Two

9 Morgan Brothers. '70s stalwarts. Richie and . . .

10 Gilo brothers a few years later, David and . . .

Wait a minute, this team has no goalie! Football formations
don't usually include a keeper, but for question 11 . . .

11 . . . can you name the Welsh international goalie who
    joined us on loan in 2011 and made no appearances?

100% City!

Time for a novelty round again now – this is a good 'un. Each of the players who make up the answers to the questions below, has been ever-present throughout an entire Football League season. So it's just a matter of identifying the stars, right. Right?

Nah, there's more to it than that of course.

We have selected an entire team of ever-presents for you to identify. Eleven players who have each appeared in 100% of City's league games throughout a complete season. See if you can solve our mystery line-up.

The formation is loosely 4-4-2 . . . starting in goal. But, given that these players are likely to be well-known to most City fans, we have made the clues a bit obscure here and there.

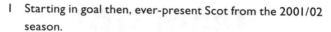

1 Starting in goal then, ever-present Scot from the 2001/02 season.

2 Yorkshire-born full-back from our 1960s days in Europe.

3 Left-back in the same line-up as 2 above.

4 Huge Scot who lined up alongside answers 2 and 3 in 42 league games back in 1970/71.

5 Ammanford-born centre half. Ever-present in 1986/87.

6 Hairy Scottish midfielder who scored a famous goal for us against Hereford United in 1976.

7 Even longer hair this time. Leading scorer and ever-present in 1986/87.

8 A diminutive, tigerish midfielder. Played for the Robins, Bluebirds and even the Baltimore Blasts . . . but never the Tigers. Arrived at Ninian Park in 1979.

9 This guy seems to crop up quite a lot in this book. Unusual feat for a man who played 3 times for Greenock Morton and now performs in Israel.

10 Ever-present up front in the same season as our ex-Greenock Morton striker.

11 A creative wing-half and inside forward who won the Welsh Cup with City in 1964 and 1965. Villa, Blackburn and hometown club Swansea also feature on his CV. (We'd probably say he played 'in the hole' these days.)

Round
24

Team GB?

As the Pride of Wales, Cardiff City can point to a long and proud record of supplying players for the national team. Some 60-plus Bluebirds have pulled on the famous red shirt for Wales.

But we have also supplied our fair share of players for the other 'home' countries down the years. Some of these have been very recent, some though . . . well, let's see how you get on. We have included Irish players in this round too for convenience.

1   Who was the first City to player to win a full England cap while playing for Cardiff City?

2   Which former England international joined us from Manchester City in 2007? He won 12 caps in total.

3   Which former City striker went on to play for England in the 1962 World Cup finals in Chile?

4   Even further back now – two City full-backs of the 1950s made England B appearances – one of them while he was at Ninian, the other after he left City. Can you name them?

5   Another two players with City connections figured for England Under-21s in the 2007 European Championship finals. One of them had recently joined Cardiff City, the other had left us a year earlier. Remember who they were?

6   Who won his 50th cap for Scotland in October 2010?

7   Who was the Scotland B defender who signed for City from Dundee in 1955?

8   Which 1920s full-back joined City from the Belfast club Crusaders, having grown up in Northern Ireland – but won his international caps for Scotland?

9   Can you recall the player who converted from goalkeeper to centre-forward, and played for City in the 2010 season, before leaving for Aberdeen? He was a Northern Ireland Under-21 international.

10 Who was the goalie who came on as a sub for the Republic of Ireland at Wembley in 1979? He was promptly lobbed by Kevin Keegan, though he was also the hero of many a relegation battle.

11 In the 2000s, which midfield general became the first City player since the above goalie to be capped for the Republic of Ireland while at Ninian Park?

Round
25

International Velvet

Football has changed, hasn't it? Back in the day, it seemed that football really was a case of 'our lot versus your lot', team line-ups hardly altered over the years and local lads featured strongly in most teams' starting XIs. Nobby Stiles played for Manchester United, Bobby Moore played for West Ham and Newport County featured all our cast-offs. These things never seemed to change. You knew who played for who. In 1967, Celtic famously won the European Cup with a team comprised entirely of Scotsmen. Indeed the entire team were all born within 30 miles of Glasgow. Unthinkable these days.

Cardiff City have always had their fair share of home-grown talent of course. From Fred Keenor, to Peter Rodrigues, Phil Dwyer, our own David Giles and more recently the likes of Chris Gunter, Aaron Ramsey and Darcy Blake. Not all Kaiirdiff Kiddies of course, but certainly well within the Bhoys' 30-mile radius.

But times, well, move on. Football these days is an international game, where stars from all corners of the world turn out for teams throughout the league. Cardiff City's first team squad for a December 2011 clash with Middlesbrough included a Frenchman who could qualify for the USA, an Irishman born in Plymouth, a Slovak, several Scotsmen, some Englishmen, and whatever-someone-born-in-Iceland-is-called. There were no Welshmen in the team at all – not even on the bench.

But let's go with it shall we? Herewith a round on the cosmopolitan celebrities of Cardiff City! China, Canada, USA . . . 'Every day when I wake up, I thank the Lord I'm a Bluebird'.

1 Cardiff City's somersaulting striker and Welsh international Robert Earnshaw was born in which country?

2 What was the birthplace of hard-running 1990s forward Cohen Griffith?

3 Ex-Stoke star (?) Kyle Lightbourne played a handful of games for us on loan in 2001. But for which country did he win caps?

4 Which 1970s left-back served as assistant manager (at the 2006 World Cup finals) for the USA?

5 Two for one here – which USA international appeared for the Bluebirds in the 2009 campaign? And who was he on a season's loan from?

6 Can you name (and pronounce!) the French striker with an unfeasibly long name who appeared on trial for City towards the end of the 2006 season?

7 Two multi-capped Oriental internationals appeared for City in the Lennie Lawrence era. Can you name them? Whether they ever played for us against Orient, who knows . . .

8　A tale of two Dutchmen – double Dutch, you might say. Anyway, one was a strapping blond centre-half, the other a right-back with an unfortunate tendency to keep turning in semi-circles. Can you name them both?

9　From Dutch to Deutsch now, remember the two frighteningly obscure Germans who featured for City during the 1990s? One was a 6ft 5in centre-half, the other an on-trial midfielder whose only game was a 4–0 defeat in a Freight Rover Trophy tie at Shrewsbury. Can you name either of them?

10　Who was the glamorous Italian who (occasionally) played up front for City in the mid-2000s?

11　Last, and probably least, in this round, which City goalies of recent years came from: Denmark, Finland and Canada?

Never Go Back

This round is all about players – and managers – for whom the lure of Ninian Park was too great. They just could not resist returning to us (you may wish some of them hadn't bothered).

1   Name the three managers who have had two (permanent) spells in charge at City.

2   And a fourth City boss, who left (for Barry Town) but then came back as caretaker-manager in the 1990s.

3   Who was the record-breaking FA Cup hero who rejoined the Bluebirds from Coventry during the ill-fated 1934 season – then quickly left again?

4   Name the pre-war goalie who left us for Wrexham in 1937 then rejoined us at the end of the war.

5 Do you recall that inside-forward in City's record-breaking 1947 side who left us for Newport County in 1948, only to return to us a year later?

6 Which striker left us for Bournemouth in 1972 then came back to us from Millwall three years later?

7 Name the left-sided player who we released as a youngster to the Welsh League. He returned to Ninian from Sheffield United in 1972.

8 Who was the fast forward who left us for Brighton in 1978 but then came back for an unexciting loan spell from Preston during our 1982 relegation season?

9 Who left us for Wrexham in 1978 and returned to us from Newport County in 1985? Legendary player. Top player. (Not that we are crawling!)

10 Who was part of a crazy 'Swap Shop' deal and left us for Newport County in 1983 but rejoined us from Gillingham a year later?

11 And lastly, can you recall the vaguely French-sounding midfielder who had not one, but two loan spells with us (from Hull City) during the 1991 season. Does he sound a bit mangey to you?

Krek Spelin pLeeZe! Harder Round

This round might be harder – not in the sense that the spellings are more difficult, but many of the players are more obscure, or are going back a bit further. So you need to really know your City to tackle this round – as well as knowing yer spelin!

1   Icelandic midfielder from the 2011/12 season.

2   Inconsistent winger or striker from the 1970s, who sounded like he should have played for Aston.

3   Another 1970s forward who never quite made it, this was a bleached-blonde Cardiff Greek whose family owned a restaurant – he had two spells with us.

4   Another 'two-speller', he was a popular utility player who captained us. Joined us from Cambridge in 1982, then again from Newport County in 1989.

5   Welsh international who joined us from Swansea in exchange for the player in question 4, in 1985 – then left us for Barry Town.

6   Goalscoring left-winger who signed from Sheffield United in 1972 – although he was originally a Cardiffian.

7   Right, they are getting a bit harder again now. Blond left-back from the late 1980s (sounded a like a platypus?).

8   Tough-tackling midfielder from the 1993 promotion side, a Northern Irishman whom we purchased from Port Vale.

9   Ginger midfielder signed from Liverpool. He made only a limited impact at Ninian Park before moving on to Barry Town.

10   Solid centre-back, ex-Fulham, who proved a popular figure after joining us from Stockport in 1996. Moved on to serve Newport County well five years later.

11   Largely unsuccessful striker, not particularly notable other than for his tongue-twisting name, who made a number of substitute appearances during a trial spell at the end of the 2006 season.

Once a Bluebird, Always a Bluebird!

After our recent heroics in the Carling Cup, we visualised many an ex-City star looking back longingly and wishing they'd stayed with us instead of seeking out greener pastures. You'll soon get the hang of it.

1   Which former City striker scored a record 11 goals in the inaugural League Cup competition in 1961 – but couldn't play in the final?

2   The 1969 final, in which Third Division Swindon Town beat Arsenal at Wembley, featured three players who later had City connections. How many of them can you name?

3   Which future City winger featured for Third Division Aston Villa in their 2–0 defeat by Spurs in the 1971 final?

4   And who captained Villa to League Cup glory in the twice-replayed final of 1977, against Everton? (Everton also had a player with City connections.)

5   Which future City boss figured in Liverpool's four consecutive successes between 1981 and 1984?

6   Which former City manager featured in the first live televised League Cup final in 1985?

7   In the 1986 final, which future Bluebird appeared for QPR in their 3–0 defeat by Oxford? (Yes, Oxford won the League Cup in 1986.)

8   Which former City youngster put on a Man of the Match display as Luton came back to beat Arsenal in the 1988 League Cup final? (Yes, Luton Town actually won the League Cup in 1988.)

9   Who scored two goals for Villa as they beat treble-chasing Manchester United in the 1994 season? (He had a loan spell at City some years earlier.)

10 Who received a League Cup losers' medal for Wigan in 2006, when the Latics were drubbed 4–0 by Manchester United?

11 And which two former City stars gained winners' medals in 2011, when Birmingham beat Arsenal 2–1?

Round 29

Pot Luck

Think of this as the general knowledge round – a random variety of City-related trivia in no particular order.

'The long, the short & the tall'

1　Who was the shortest player to play in the league for Cardiff City – and who was the tallest?

2　Even more random now. Which players had the longest and shortest names? We are not counting middle names here, only the players' commonly used names – but you can get an extra point if you remember a City player who had a load of middle names.

'United nations'

3　Can you name three Cardiff City players whose surnames are also the names of countries?

'Oggie O.G. Oggie!'

4 Which Cardiff City player scored more own goals for
   City – or rather, against City – than anyone else – 14, in
   fact, in 6 seasons (1955–61)?

5 A more recent City centre-half scored two 'oggies' in
   only 5 league appearances during the early 2000s. Who
   was he, then?

'Class dismissed'

6 Who was the only City player to be sent off on his debut?

7 Who was sent off twice in his 20 appearances back in the
   mid-1970s (he had a host of bookings too).

'They left it late'

8 One game, one goal. A sensational winner against Wigan
   in 1982 to clinch a 3–2 home victory. That would be?

9 This guy will probably always come last in any A–Z of
   Cardiff City. Australian keeper. Another one-game
   wonder.

'1927 and all that'

10 Who was the manager when Cardiff City won the FA
    Cup?

11 On which date did Cardiff City win the FA Cup? We
    mean the specific date.

30

And Finally . . .

We have finally reached the end of the road, the long and winding road. We don't mean the long walk down Ninian Park Road to the railway station, or even – for those of you who have stuck with this book since the introduction – the M6 to Preston. We mean of course, the last pages of this quiz.

So, in keeping with the theme, the last round of the book is all about famous endings, last days and closures. The end of the line. Though there's always *Never Mind the Bluebirds 2* of course!

An obvious one to start, but they get tougher.

1   Who were Cardiff City's opponents in the last ever league game at Ninian Park?

2   What was Brian Clark's last competitive appearance for Cardiff City – and what was strange about the game?

3   Who was the last native Cardiffian to manage Cardiff City?

4   Who were Cardiff City's opponents in their last pre-war league fixture? (Second World War that is.)

5   Phil Dwyer's last appearance for Cardiff City came against which famous old club?

6   John Toshack's last goal for Cardiff City at Ninian Park came against which opponents?

7   After beating Cardiff City on aggregate in a two-legged semi-final, who were the last English winners of the Welsh Cup in 1990?

8   On 28 April 2007, Aaron Ramsey came on as substitute against Hull City to replace Paul Parry and thus became Cardiff City's youngest ever player aged 16 years and 124 days. Prior to this, who was the last player to hold this record for Cardiff City?

9   Craig Bellamy, Prince of Wales, made his last appearance for Cardiff City against which royal opponents prior to his 'second coming' in 2012?

10 Next we ask you to name the nation against which Jason Perry won the last of his one caps for Wales in 1994 at Ninian Park?

11 And finally, we end with our own small tribute to the late Gary Speed. In a match played at Cardiff City Stadium on 12 November 2011, who were Wales' opponents in Gary Speed's last game in charge?

The 'Current Affairs' Round

1 Kenny Miller.
2 23 (Bend it Like Darcy?).
3 West Bromwich Albion.
4 We were booted out by the Cobblers – Northampton Town.
5 Mark Hudson – something of a tap-in by his standards.
6 Aaron Ramsey, in Cardiff of course.
7 Joe Mason (red) and Aron Gunnarsson (blue).

8 Jimmy Andrews.

9 Ben qualifies for the Land of his Fathers via his Welsh grandmother. He was born in Birmingham.

10 From Brighton & Hove Albion. Bargain.

11 Here goes…

Miller (hit post)
Cowie (scored)
Whittingham (scored)
Gestade (hit post)
Gerrard (don't even go there . . .)

Singing the Blues

1   Peter Thorne (striker – 51 goals between 2001 and 2005).

Peter Thorne is magic
He wears a magic hat
And when he signed for Cardiff
He said, 'I fancy that!'
He wouldn't sign for Wrexham or Jack B*stards 'cos
    they're shite
He signed for Cardiff City 'cos they're f**king DYNAMITE!

2   Jeff Hemmerman – goalscoring hero turned physio . . . look!

Hemmerman. Hemmerman. Jeffrey Hemmerman.
He gets the ball and scores a goal.
Jeffrey Hemmerman!

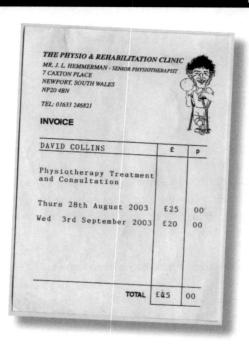

THE PHYSIO & REHABILITATION CLINIC
MR. J. L. HEMMERMAN - SENIOR PHYSIOTHERAPIST
7 CAXTON PLACE
NEWPORT, SOUTH WALES
NP20 4BN

TEL: 01633 246821

INVOICE

DAVID COLLINS	£	p
Physiotherapy Treatment and Consultation		
Thurs 28th August 2003	£25	00
Wed 3rd September 2003	£20	00
TOTAL	£45	00

3 Nathan Blake – 1990s legend.

He's black
He's mean
He robs the fruit machine
Nathan Blake, Nathan Blake!

4 Phil Stant – 11 goals in 1992/93.

Who needs Cantona?
When we've got Stant-ona!

5 Stan Richards – 30 league goals in 1946/47. This chant was based on the popular song of the day 'Open the door Richard', an amusing ditty sprinkled with references to aspects of urban African-American life.

Open the score Richards – and nod one in.

6 Tony Evans – the ultimate 1970s hero, moustache, sideburns, the lot . . .

Tony Evans Walks on water
La la la, la-la, la la la-la.

7 Craig Bellamy.

Craig Bellamy's magic
He wears a magic hat
And when he signed for Cardiff
He said, 'I fancy that!'
He wouldn't sign for Celtic 'cos Joe Ledley said they're
**   shite,**
He signed for Cardiff City 'cos they're f**king DYNAMITE!

8 Kevin McNaughton – excellent recent favourite. Lyrics have been slightly rewritten since we first heard this ditty at Derby in August 2010. Here is the original:

Oh Kev McNaughton – You are the love of my life.
Oh Kev McNaughton – I'd let you sleep with my wife
Oh Kev McNaughton – I want silver hair too!

9 Michael Chopra.

What's that coming over the hill?
It's Michael Chopra . . . it's Michael Chopraaa!

10 George Wood (keeper from the 1980s – ex-Arsenal).

Georgie Wood,
Georgie Wood.
Georgie, Georgie Wood.
He's got no hair but we don't care,
Georgie, Georgie Wood.

11 Jason Perry.

You're Supposed to Be at Home!

1   1910.

2   Lord Ninian Crichton-Stuart, son of the Marquis of Bute and one of the club's benefactors. He also 'kicked off' the first game at the new ground.

3   Aston Villa.

4   The famous Captain Morgan logo was visible (just!) from 1960 until 1992 – 32 years.

5   The roof was removed in 1977 but replaced in 2000.

6   The original Grandstand (which spanned the length of the pitch) was burned down in a fire in 1937. A much smaller, 'matchbox' Grandstand replaced it. The new Grandstand replaced the matchbox in 1973.

7 The 'Blue Dragons' arrived on the scene in 1981.
8 Howard Winstone fought Vicente Saldivar for the featherweight championship in 1967.
9 Bob Marley . . . with his Wailers, of course.
10 Pope John Paul II.
11 Many City fans would have known Phil Suarez as the radio commentator on CBC, Red Dragon and Real Radio. But, to answer the question, Phil was also the announcer at Ninian Park as well as the internet commentator for a while. Phil sadly lost his battle against cancer in September 2002.

1   Bell.
2   Liverpool.
3   Loovens.
4   Scoular.
5   Riverside.
6   Earnie.

7   Elsey.
8   Young.
9   Grangetown.
10 Neal.
11 Lynex.
12 X . . . errm . . . errrm . . .

Round

5

Early Days

1 Bartley Wilson.
2 Riverside AFC.
3 Chocolate and Amber!
4 Sophia Gardens – with occasional appearances at The Harlequins ground just behind Newport Road.
5 1908.
6 Jack Evans. (Be honest, did you really know that?)
7 Trixie.
8 Fred Stewart –managed City from 1911 until 1933.
9 Cup-final goalscorer Hughie Ferguson (by now playing for Dundee) committed suicide.
10 The Grandstand burned down.
11 Huddersfield Town, who went on to win the league three times in a row (the first club to do so). City actually finished level on points and lost the title on goal average.

Bluebirds Bad Boys

1 Robin Friday. Friday's amazing antics are told in Paul McGuigan's book, *The Greatest Footballer You Never Saw*. The same McGuigan ('Guigsy') who was the bassist with Oasis from 1991 to 1999, by the way. It's definitely maybe the same guy.
2 Keith Robson.
3 Craig Bellamy.
4 Michael Chopra.

5   Nathan Blake.
6   Linden Jones.
7   Leon Jeanne.
8   Christian Roberts.
9   Steve McPhail.
10 Robin Friday (we thought he deserved two entries!).
11 Dai Thomas.

Pride of Wales

1   22 times.
2   We are one behind Wrexham, on 23. Swansea are in third, but way back on 10 wins.
3   At Swansea's illustrious former ground, the Vetch Field. The dribbling goalscorer was former darling of the Vetch Alan Curtis (heh heh).

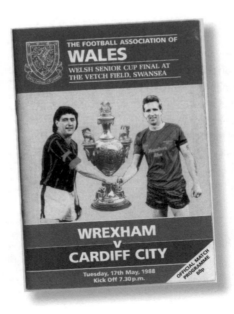

4 Latham played after City's regular defender Bob Lawrie made a late withdrawal. City beat Pontypridd Town 2–0, and Latham gave his winner's medal to Lawrie. Sealey gave his FA Cup medal to Jim Leighton after the 1990 FA Cup final replay, in which he had replaced Leighton.

5 They won it, beating Rhyl 2–0 in the final at Wrexham.

6 1992 – City beat Hednesford Town 1–0.

7 Hereford United (then a Southern League side), Stourbridge and the aforementioned Hednesford Town – who are located in Staffordshire (not far from Chasetown).

8 For throwing mud at each other!

9 Because the body of Swansea's Alan Davies was discovered on the morning of the match, the player having committed suicide.

10 Carl Dale – close-range header past Wrexham's Andy Marriott.

11 The National Stadium. We will accept Cardiff Arms Park but not the answer 'the Millennium Stadium'. The National Stadium was demolished in 1997. The Millennium Stadium is a new ground so it doesn't count!

Robbie Fowler

1 Liverpool (Robbie started off at Anfield of course before moving to Leeds and Manchester City, but he returned to the Kop in 2006 and joined us the following year).
2 West Bromwich Albion.
3 None.
4 Steve McManaman.
5 God. He was also known as the Toxteth Terror at times.

John Charles

1 Leeds.
2 Hereford United.
3 38.
4 AS Roma (1962–3).
5 Jeremy Charles.

Gerry Francis

1 12.
2 8 (a surprisingly high proportion).
3 2nd – runners-up to Liverpool.
4 7.

5   Francis scored the goal of the season for QPR against Liverpool
    in 1975 and is also remembered for his two-goal show while
    captaining England to a 5–1 victory over Scotland at Wembley
    in the same year. Sadly, he never found the net for us.

Craig Bellamy

1   Bobby Robson.
2   PFA Young Player of the Year.
3   Sierra Leone.
4   Norwich City.
5   The keeper was Gianluigi Buffon.

Kevin Ratcliffe

1   Carlisle United.
2   Belgium.
3   Watford.
4   Neville Southall.
5   Chester City (now defunct) and Shrewsbury Town. He joins
    a long line of top class players who never really succeeded in
    management.

Mike England

1   Harold!
2   Blackburn Rovers.
3   The Shay, Halifax.
4   None.
5   New England Tea Men (as opposed to the Mike England Tea
    Men).

The Road to Wembley

1   Once, back in 1927 of course. We couldn't get a ticket, sadly.

2   3 times (1925, 1927 and 2008).

3   4 times . . . the three finals and the 2008 semi-final against Barnsley.

4   Scott Young v Leeds and Nathan Blake against Manchester City in 1994. Peter Sayer grabbed the only goal in our 1–0 victory over Spurs back in 1977 – a goal that featured extensively on *Match of the Day*.

5   1921, 1925, 1927 and 2008.

6   Chasetown was the lowest-ranked club ever to reach the third round of the FA Cup. It's in Staffordshire.

7 A second leg! Because league football had not yet resumed after the interruption of the war, it was decided that the FA Cup that year (and only that year) would be on a two-legged basis, up to and including the quarter-finals.

8 Peter Whittingham (with his right foot) and Roger Johnson (with a diving header from a free-kick).

9 Phil Stant (a header) and Nathan Blake (a tame shot which wriggled through the hands of Boro' keeper Steve Pears).

10 Enfield Town. We beat them 4–1 away in the second round in 1988/89, then we drew 0–0 away in 1993/94 (first round), beating them 1–0 at Ninian in the replay. We we lost 1–0 away to them in the first round the following season – third time unlucky!

11 Ton Pentre. City travelled the short distance up the Rhondda, and came away with a 4–1 win. Alan Curtis played for us against his hometown team!

Jeux Sans Frontières

1 1964 against Esbjerg of Denmark.
2 They beat Esbjerg and Sporting Lisbon before bowing out
   to Real Zaragoza at the quarter-final stage.
3 Three times – 1967, 1973 and 1976.
4 1968, semi-final. We lost to SV Hamburg in a famous Ninian
   Park encounter.
5 Owing to a big freeze in Moscow the away leg was played in
   Tashkent, in what is now Uzbekistan (we didn't go).

6 Augsburg, Bavaria, Germany. Two draws meant that a replay was needed – no 'away goals count double' in those days.

7 Pezoporikos Larnaca (Cyprus) and Nantes.

8 Jimmy Gilligan. Derry City represented the Republic of Ireland, even though they are based in Northern Ireland.

9 We went out to Aarhus – 'Aarhus . . . in the middle of Aar Street.' Oh come on, you have to allow us one corny one!

10 Standard Liège of Belgium. We lost 5–2 away with Tony Bird scoring twice. The home leg also ended in defeat, 3–1 this time with a goal from the late Robbie James.

11 Real Madrid won 2–0 to take the tie 2–1 on aggregate.

Connect 4

Connect I

1 Aaron Ramsey.
2 Mel Charles.
3 George Wood.
4 Jay-Emmanuel Thomas.

Connection I – Arsenal

Ramsey left us for Arsenal, Mel Charles and George Wood each played for Arsenal before they joined us, while the Gunners also loaned us JET in 2010/11.

Connect 2

1 Jimmy Gilligan.
2 Frank Burrows.
3 Gary O'Neil.
4 Paul Went.

Connection 2 – Portsmouth

Jimmy Gilligan moved to Pompey from Ninian Park in 1989, Frankie Burrows managed the south coast outfit, while Gary O'Neil and Paul Went were both signed by Cardiff City from Portsmouth.

Arsenal

ARSENAL FOOTBALL CLUB
HIGHBURY HOUSE
75 DRAYTON PARK
LONDON N5 1BU

TELEPHONE: +44 (0)20 7704 4000
FAX: +44 (0)20 7704 4001
E-MAIL: info@arsenal.co.uk
www.arsenal.com

FA YOUTH CUP 6th ROUND
ARSENAL V CARDIFF CITY
MONDAY 19 FEBRUARY 2007
AT EMIRATES STADIUM
KICK OFF: 7.00 PM

ARSENAL		CARDIFF CITY
Lee BUTCHER	1	
Abumere OGOGO	2	Josh HERRING
Paul RODGERS	3	James SIMPSON
Gavin HOTE	4	Matt SMITH
Rene STEER	5	Jack CARLISLE
James DUNNE	6	Lloyd EVANS
Mark RANDALL	7	Bradley MIDDLETON
Francisco MERIDA-PEREZ	8	Jon BROWN
Kieran GIBBS	9	Aaron RAMSEY
Nacer BARAZITE	10	Mark JONES
Jay SIMPSON	11	James UPCOTT
		Kyle BASSETT
Giorgos EFREM	12	
Wojciech SZCZESNY	13	TBC
Vincent VAN DEN BERG	14	TBC
Jay THOMAS	15	TBC
Henri LANSBURY	16	TBC
		TBC

Manager: Steve Bould

Manager:

OFFICIALS: Referee:
            Assistant Referees: S J Bratt
                                       G D Horwood
            4th Official: G J N Jerden
                                       G S Evetts

FORTHCOMING MATCH AT EMIRATES:

Arsenal v Reading
Barclaycard Premier League
Saturday 3rd March
Kick Off 3pm

willow
foundation
speed closer for seriously ill young adults
ARSENAL CHARITY 2006/2007
Registered Charity No.1106746

The Arsenal Football Club Plc - Company Registration Number 109244 England

Connect 3

1 Dave Powell.
2 Gil Reece.
3 Mel Rees.
4 Nathan Blake.

Connection 3 – Sheffield United

Powell and Gil Reece joined City from the Blades and Mel Rees
had a spell at Bramall Lane, as did Nathan Blake, though we
understand Nathan retains little affection for United these days!

Connect 4

1 Ian Walsh.
2 Jon Parkin is from Barnsley.
3 Billy Ronson.
4 Gordon Owen.

Connection 4 – Barnsley

Walshie had a spell at Barnsley between stints as a Jack and a
Bluebird. He is now a BBC Wales regular of course. Barnsley is
Jon Parkin's hometown club and Billy Ronson later spent 4 years

at Barnsley after leaving us for Wrexham in 1981. Gordon Owen was born in Barnsley and, like Ronson, also left us for Barnsley in 1984 (were things so bad in Cardiff in the 1980s that Barnsley was more attractive?).

Connect the Connections

So, we have Arsenal, Portsmouth, Sheffield United and Barnsley, what is the overall connection between these connections? Well, of course, they are the four teams City have met in the FA Cup at Wembley – Arsenal (1927), Portsmouth (2008), Sheffield United (1925) and Barnsley (2008). Easy when you know how, eh?

A Cup by Any Other Name . . .

1 The semi-finals, in 1966. We played First Division West Ham in a two-legged semi, in which we were crushed 5–2 away, then 5–1 at home. So a 10–3 aggregate defeat – our heaviest-ever loss in this competition. Our excuse was that three West Ham players went on to feature in England's World Cup win at the end of the season.

2 David Yorath – anyone remember him? Brother of Terry.

3 Tony Evans.

4 George Wood.

5 By Luton Town's decision to ban away fans from the tie, to be played at Kenilworth Road. The League ruled that this was out of order, and kicked Luton out of the competition – so City went through. You'll never ban a City fan!

6 Chelsea, 2–1 at Ninian Park.

7   Bobby Smith, who was caretaker-manager for one game in between the departure of Frank Burrows and the return of Len Ashurst.

8   Northampton Town. They beat us over two legs at the start of the season, then beat us over two legs at the end of the season, in the play-off semi-final.

9   Wimbledon and Crystal Palace – both away ties were played at Selhurst Park.

10 Boston United.

11 At Anfield, to Liverpool. City lost 2–1 and Darren Purse scored our goal. Our next encounter with the Anfield boys came at Wembley in 2012.

Dad or Chips

(Not surprisingly . . . this bit took us the longest!)

	David	Gareth
1	Away.	Me too (as long as I can navigate).
2	To follow!	Mackay.
3	I have to say Earnie (my son would never forgive me).	Earnie. Picking Chops would be too much of a gamble.
4	Joe.	Jason Perry!
5	Black.	Yellow.
6	Ooooh . . .	That's an easy one, Dave . . . promotion!
7	Cymru.	City (who are 'Wales'?).

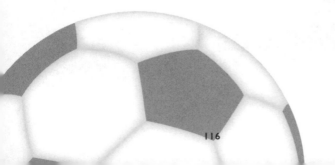

	David	**Gareth**
8	On the side.	Depends. Are we home or away?
9	Ninian Park.	Ninian. Not worth asking really.
10	The Liberty (the posh bits are very nice).	The Vetch (as in 'retch').
11	Message boards (sorry Gareth).	Fanzines. What are 'message boards' exactly?
12	Standing.	Yeah, standing. You can get cramp sitting down – plus it's easier to walk out.
13	Hemmerman.	Gilligan.
14	Tosh.	Clark. Better pies too.
15	Only Cardiff City . . . 'Do The Ayatollah'	'The Ayatollah, which has become our trademark.
16	Burkey!	Burke!
17	Frankie.	Frankly Frankie, to be frank.
18	The mighty Bob Bank.	Ditto.
19	Parry.	Custard creams.
20	Bellamy.	Kylie.

Derby Delights

1   True! After over 500 games, the Cardiff City legend had a 5-game loan spell at Swansea in 1974.

2   Nah, false of course. But there was interest way out west as Big Joe's days at Cardiff drew to a close in the 1980s. Not sure we could have stomached that.

3   Quicker than that I am afraid – Leigh Barnard scored after only 45 seconds in 1989, so it's false.

4   Very true. 1980 for Swansea in the famous 3–3 Boxing Day Christmas cracker, and for Cardiff City in a less well-remembered encounter against the Jacks in the Sherpa Van Trophy. John Toshack and Jimmy Gilligan are others to have performed the same feat.

5 False. The Gentle Giant joined the Vetch Field ground staff after leaving school but he never actually played for Swansea. He went to Leeds in 1949. Later he joined us of course, in 1963.

6 False. Big Tosh never managed Cardiff City – though he had a one-game spell in the Ninian Park dug-out as manager of Wales against Norway in 1994.

7 False again sorry. Ex-Swansea boss Terry Yorath also had a stint as Bluebirds manager between November 1994 and March 1995. Others to have had the pleasure include Trevor Morris and Billy McCandless.

8 False. Only David did so, Paul had stints at Cardiff, Newport and even Merthyr, but never enjoyed the 'pleasure' of playing for the Swans.

9 True! A January 1944 clash saw tough tackling, a pitch invasion and an attempted attack on City defender Fred Stansfield by a Swansea fan. Who says football hooliganism is a 1980s invention, eh? Only 3,500 there for that fiery wartime encounter too.

10 False. Season 2010/11, a Craig Bellamy cracker saw City gain the spoils in a famous 1–0 victory (had to get that one in!).

11 False. Bizarrely Swansea chose to wear red shirts with black shorts and socks. Quite why this should have been so has defeated us. We even asked Gilo but he could shed no light on it. It was too early for the replica shirt craze and there would have been no clash between Swansea's usual white and the all blue ensemble worn by Cardiff City that day. Just goes to show, not even we have all the answers.

The Swinging Sixties

1 Aston Villa; the scorer was Graham Moore.
2 54,000 – it was the biggest crowd in the entire Football League that Saturday.
3 Alan Durban.
4 Steve Gammon. And he really was hurt – he wasn't hamming it up.
5 10,000. Awful!
6 John Charles, signed from Roma (not Juventus!).
7 Bradford Park Avenue, often known as Bradford PA. They produced better secretaries than players . . .
8 Greg Farrell. The game is nearly always referred to as 'Greg Farrell's game'.
9 David Summerhayes, against Bury.
10 West Ham United and SV Hamburg.
11 Blackpool, Huddersfield Town and Wolves.

The Biggest and the Best

1 Aston Villa. A crowd of around 7,000 saw City lose a specially arranged friendly 2–0. Lord Ninian Crichton-Stuart took the kick-off to officially open the ground.

2 Clark 79, Toshack 77. Almost too close to call.

3 Tom Farquharson, 481. Made his debut against Manchester United in 1922 – that was even before Fergie's time!

4 Don Murray made 33 appearances in the European Cup Winners' Cup.

5 31.

6 Derek Tapscott scored 6 against Knighton Town in the fifth round of the Welsh Cup in 1961 as City won 16–0! We have heard unconfirmed rumours that sections of the crowd began singing 'We want 17 . . .'.

7 Len Davies, 7 hat-tricks in total. Probably best remembered though, for a crucial penalty against Huddersfield. Len's spot-kick was saved, which led to us missing out on the 1924 league championship on goal difference. We have never come as close since.

8 John Buchanan scored the 8 goals.

9 Graham Kavanagh, signed in 2001 from Stoke City.

10 The answer for question 10 is . . . 10. He even wore the number 10 shirt in 1978 to score against England at Ninian Park!

11 King Kenny Miller.

Krek Spelin pLeeZe!

1 Kevin McNaughton.
2 Peter Enckelman.
3 Josh Magennis.
4 Glenn Loovens.
5 Jason Koumas.
6 Riccy Scimeca. Known earlier in his career as 'Riccardo Scimeca' but you don't need to know that.
7 Gabor Gyepes.
8 Seyi Olofinjana.
9 Junichi Inamoto.
10 Martyn Margetson – note the odd spelling of 'Martyn'.
11 Dimi Konstantopoulos. Although his full first name is actually 'Dimitrios' – but we won't pester you for that!

McBluebirds

1 Don Cowie.

2 David Marshall.

3 No, not Kev McNaughton! It was Paul Quinn.

4 Steven Thompson, Gavin Rae and Chris Burke.

5 John Buchanan.

6 Don Murray.

7 Danny Malloy.

8 Hughie Ferguson.

9 Jimmy Blair.

10 Going backwards: Malky Mackay, Frank Burrows (twice), Jimmy Andrews, Jimmy Scoular and City's first professional manager, Davy McDougall (in 1910/11).

11 Aberdeen (Kevin McNaughton), Northampton Town (John Buchanan), Celtic (Freddie Pethard), Kirkintilloch Rob Roy (Jim Eadie) and Arbroath (Alec Milne). The extra point – John Buchanan also played for Ross County.

Anoraknophobia!

1 The Fred Keenor Challenge Cup – City lost 2–1.

2 The Anglo-Scottish Cup, in 1978/79.

3 They played Bristol Rovers away (lost 1–0), Fulham at home (won 1–0), and Bristol City away (lost 1–0). All games were played in August 1978 and Phil Dwyer scored our only goal.

4 It was played neither in Cardiff nor Hamilton, but in the more northern town of Perth – 'behind closed doors', where City reportedly (or reputedly) won 1–0. Spooky!

5 The 1927 Football Association Charity Shield match was held at Stamford Bridge, home of Chelsea. Cardiff City, as cup winners, met amateur side Corinthians. The game ended in a 2–1 win for Cardiff City with the winning goal scored by Hughie Ferguson. Later that season City also met the Scottish Cup winners Celtic, but lost heavily.

6 Nottingham Forest.

7 Stoke City (Phil Dwyer), Wolves (Ron Healey), Manchester United (Harry Parsons) and Spurs (Jason Perry).

8 Gavin Gordon.

9 Gavin Gordon, again.

10 Mainly the tour was in Australia, but one game was in New Zealand, and the opening game was in New Caledonia, which is an overseas territory of France.

11 Trevor Morris.

Round

20

Cum On Feel the Noize!

1 Toshack and Clark of course (John Toshack and Brian Clark).
2 Ian Gibson.
3 Frank O'Farrell.
4 Phil Dwyer. He swallowed his tongue following a collision on the pitch at Gillingham, but his life was saved by the City physio – see the next batch of answers for the physio's name!
5 Crystal Palace and Carlisle United.
6 Tony Villars in the Palace game, and Alan Campbell versus Carlisle. City came from behind to draw on both occasions.
7 Willie Anderson, who joined us not from Manchester United (where he had begun his career) but Aston Villa.
8 Adrian Alston, who had played for Australia; we signed him from Luton Town.
9 The late Jimmy Andrews.
10 The Hereford attendance was around 35,000. Malcolm Allison, manager of promotion rivals Palace, had predicted to the media that Palace would get more for their next home game than City. He was proven wrong!
11 Jimmy Scoular, Frank O'Farrell, Jimmy Andrews and Richie Morgan. Their 'number twos' were Lew Clayton, Jimmy Andrews, Alan Sealey and Brian Harris.

1 Gary Stevens and Ronnie Moore. (Stevens and Moore – not quite the same ring as Toshack and Clark!)

2 Willie Carlin – and he was our best player in that half-season.

3 Lance Hayward.

4 Ron Durham.

5 In chronological order, City finished 5th, 7th and 3rd.

6 Bury. We used to play Bury a lot in those days (think of that when you next cry 'Sack the Board!' because we have slumped at home against West Ham).

7 A 7–1 defeat. Annoying . . .

8 Keith Barber.

9 Bill Irwin made the 'Save of the Season' against Leeds (in the FA Cup); Peter Sayer scored the goal against Spurs (also in an FA Cup tie).

10 The Grange-Enders, whose drummer was Alan Giles – father of David and Paul.

11   Nicknames. Here we go:

Phil Dwyer was Joe because his team-mates thought he
    looked like Joe Royle.

Showers was Danny since he looked like Danny from
    TV's *The Partridge Family*, though we have also heard
    reference to him resembling Danny Kaye.

Linden 'the Werewolf' Jones (after his scary beard).

Rod 'The Fox' Thomas (was he canny, or just looked a bit
    like one?).

Ray Bishop was 'The Ferret' – we are not sure why,
    probably because he was always scavenging for chances.
    Or maybe people used to stuff him down their trousers?

Four-Four Two

Jason **Brown**

Steve **Derrett**

Gavin **Rae**

David **Giles**

Ross **McCormack**

Jimmy **Gilligan**

Alan **Warboys**

Robert **Earnshaw**

Hughie **Ferguson**
(1926, 1927, 1928 and 1929)

Peter **Morgan**

Paul **Giles**

100% City!

1 Neil **Alexander**

2 Dave **Carver**

4 Don **Murray**

5 Terry **Boyle**

3 Gary **Bell**

6 Alan **Campbell**

7 Paul **Wimbleton**

8 Billy **Ronson**

11 Barrie **Hole**

9 Robert **Earnshaw**
(okay, 6 of these
were as a sub)

10 Peter **Thorne**

Team GB?

1   Jay Bothroyd, of course. They are not all this easy, mind.
2   Trevor Sinclair, formerly of QPR and West Ham.
3   Gerry Hitchens.
4   Charlie Rutter (while he was at City) and Jack Mansell (after he left us for Portsmouth).
5   Peter Whittingham (who had just joined us) appeared as an over-age player, and Cameron Jerome, who had left us for Birmingham City, also featured in the squad.
6   Kenny Miller.
7   Danny Malloy.
8   Jimmy Nelson.
9   Josh Magennis.
10 The great Ron Healey.
11 Oooh ahh . . . Graham Kavanagh.

Round 25 · International Velvet

1 Zambia. His family later moved to Malawi – and then on to Caerphilly. Exotic, eh?
2 Guyana.
3 Bermuda.
4 Clive Charles.
5 Eddie Johnson, on loan from Fulham. 'U-S-A! U-S-A!'
6 Guylain Ndumbu-Nsungu. Altogether now, 'Give us a G . . .'
7 Fan Zhiyi, the China captain; and Junichi Inamoto (known as 'Moto') of Japan.
8 Glenn Loovens and Winston Faerber – anyone remember him? Thought not!
9 The centre-half was Jörn Schwinkendorf; the midfielder was the unforgettable Mario Meithig. Or was it Miethig?
10 The almost equally memorable Andrea Ferretti. This Common Market malarkey has done us a power of good.
11 Kasper Schmeichel; Peter Enckelman; and Jordan Santiago.

(Phew . . . glad that round's out of the way. The spellchecker can't cope with it!)

1   Cyril Spiers, Len Ashurst and Frank Burrows.
2   Eddie May.
3   Ernie Curtis, who had been the youngest player ever to appear in an FA Cup final.
4   George Poland.
5   Bryn Allen.
6   Brian Clark.
7   Gil Reece.
8   Peter Sayer.
9   David Giles.
10 Tarki Micallef.
11 Ken De Mange.

Krek Spelin pLeeZe! Harder Round

27

1 Aron Gunnarsson.
2 Tony Villars.
3 Tarki Micallef.
4 Roger Gibbins.
5 Chris Marustik.
6 Gil Reece. The 'Gil' was short for Gilbert, actually, but you don't need to know that to get your point.
7 Nicky Platnauer.
8 Paul Millar.
9 Layton Maxwell. Note the cunning spelling of his first name! (Our spelling is according to the City programmes of his time at Ninian. However, he is listed in Wikipedia as 'Leyton'. In the interests of fair play, either spelling will get you a point. But definitely not 'Leighton'!)
10 Jeff Eckhardt.
11 Guylain Ndumbu-Nsungu.

1 Gerry Hitchens. Villa couldn't play the final during the 1961 season due to fixture congestion (they played a number of replays – hence Hitch's high number of goals). By the time they played Rotherham at the start of the following season, Hitch had been sold to Inter Milan. His record of 11 was eventually broken by Clive Allen of Spurs (with 12) in the 1987 season.

2 For Swindon, Rod Thomas and Frankie Burrows figured in defence. Arsenal's goal was scored by fox-in-the-box striker Bobby Gould.

3 Willie Anderson.

4 Briton Ferry's finest, Leighton Phillips. The Everton right-back (in the first game only) was one Dave Jones. Whatever became of him, eh?

5 Phil Neal.

6 Len Ashurst, manager of beaten Sunderland – beaten despite a 'Man of the Match' display from our former centre-back Gary Bennett.

7 Robbie James.

8 Andy Dibble, sometimes known as Andrew Dibble – and sometimes as 'Officer Dibble'.

9 Dean Saunders. The ref was Keith Cooper of Tonypandy.

10 Graham Kavanagh.

11 Roger Johnson and Cameron Jerome (the latter came on as substitute).

Pot Luck

I   The shortest – Brian Flynn at 5ft 3½in. Willie Carlin (early
    1970s midfield general), Paul Brayson (2000s forward)
    and Alan Wright (on-loan left-back from 2007) are all
    listed as being 5ft 4in – 4in shorter than Robert Earnshaw,
    incidentally.

    As for the tallest, this is probably the German defender
    Jörn Schwinkendorf, who played for us a few times in
    1999/2000, and stood at 6ft 5in – an inch taller than Ben
    Turner, Seyi Olofinjana and Leo Fortune-West. This seems
    to be taller than any of our goalkeepers, of whom the tallest
    has probably been Tony Warner, at 6ft 4in.

2   Shortest name – Paul Went (1970s utility man), at eight
    letters (one less than Paul Giles). Of course there was
    Quincy (six letters), but he does have a surname of Owusu-
    Abeyie (although he doesn't always use it), which kind of

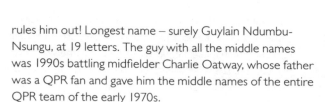

rules him out! Longest name – surely Guylain Ndumbu-Nsungu, at 19 letters. The guy with all the middle names was 1990s battling midfielder Charlie Oatway, whose father was a QPR fan and gave him the middle names of the entire QPR team of the early 1970s.

3 Mike England is the most obvious, also Derek Brazil and pre-war and post-war goalie George Poland.

4 The real 'OG King' was inspiring skipper Danny Malloy. In his day, shots that took a deflection were not claimed by the forward, and were credited (or debited!) to the unfortunate defender.

5 The unforgettable Andy Jordan, son of Joe. Oh – you had forgotten him already?

6 Right-back Phil Bater was sent off at Wrexham in September 1987.

7 The late Robin Friday.

8 Billy Woof.

9 Peter Zois.

10 Fred Stewart.

11 23 April (St George's Day).

And Finally . . .

1 Ipswich Town.

2 It was the 1976 Welsh Cup final against Hereford, first leg. Clark scored in a 3–2 win at Ninian Park. Bizarrely the game was played after the second leg because Hereford had fielded an ineligible player when the game was first played, so Clarky's goal came in the 'replay'. Or was it the first leg . . . no, the second . . . no wait . . . oh, you know what we mean!

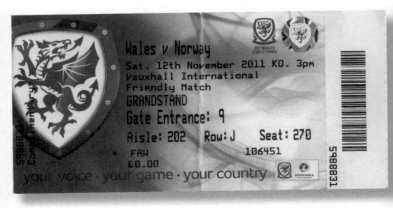

Wales v Norway

Sat. 12th November 2011 KO. 3pm
Vauxhall International
Friendly Match
GRANDSTAND
Gate Entrance: 9
Aisle: 202   Row: J   Seat: 270
FAW   106451
£0.00

your voice · your game · your country

3   Terry Yorath was born in Cardiff on 27 March 1950 and
    took over the hot seat from Eddie May in November 1994.
    He was also a director and part of a consortium that was
    seeking to buy the club. He resigned in 1995. Was he a
    'proper' manager we hear you say? Okay, you can have
    Richie Morgan for good measure.

4   Cardiff City lost 4–2 at home to Notts County on
    2 September 1939. Hitler had invaded Poland the day
    before.

5   Again, Notts County. On 17 March 1985 Cardiff City lost
    4–1 at Meadow Lane.

6   This famous goal completed Toshack's hat-trick in a 5–0
    victory over Hull City.

7   Hereford United, who beat Wrexham 2–1 in the final.

8   John Toshack.

9   Reading. 2011. Play-off disaster.

10 Norway.

11 Again, Norway.

Bibliography

As we stated at the beginning of this book, this is all our own work. We have relied on our own knowledge, gained from long years on the open terraces of Ninian Park, comfier times at the Cardiff City Stadium, countless away trips and a thousand post-match drinks. We are content that these experiences provide a body of research upon which the reader can rely.

Just to be sure though, we have occasionally consulted other historical sources to corroborate information, check dates and spellings or even just settle arguments between ourselves. The following, in no particular order, are examples of books and publications, which we, as authors have found to be reliable. We happily recommend these works to any fan of Cardiff City AFC. The Greatest Team in Football, The World Has Ever Seen . . .

Citizen (Dewi Lewis), *The Cardiff City Story* (*South Wales Echo*,
    Cardiff, editions in 1947, 1952 & 1960)

Collins, David, *Born Under a Grange End Star: The life and loves of
    a Cardiff City fan*, Sigma Leisure, Ammanford, 2002

Clark, Brian, with Shepherd, Richard, *Real, Robins & Bluebirds:
    The Autobiography of 'Goal Scorer' Brian Clark*, Vertical
    Editions, Skipton, 2006

Crooks, John, *Cardiff City Chronology, 1920–86*, self-published,
    Pontypool, 1986

Hayes, Dean, *Cardiff City Football Club: An A–Z*, Aureus, Cardiff,
    1998

———, *The South Wales Derbies: A History of Cardiff City versus
    Swansea City*, The Parrs Wood Press, Manchester, 2003

———, *The Who's Who of Cardiff City*, Breedon Books, Derby,
    2006

Jackson, Peter, *The Cardiff City Story*, S.A. Brain & Co., Cardiff, 1974

Jenkins, Derrick, & Stennett, Ceri, *Wembley 1927: The Cardiff-Arsenal FA Cup Final 1927*, self-published, Cardiff, 1989

Lloyd, Grahame, *C'mon City! A Hundred Years of the Bluebirds*, Seren, Bridgend, 1999

Morgan, Dennis, *Farewell to Ninian Park*, self-published, Cardiff, 2008

Shepherd, Richard, *Cardiff City Miscellany*, Pitch Publishing, Brighton, 2007

Tapscott, Derek, with Grandin, Terry, *Tappy: from Barry Town to Arsenal, Cardiff City and Beyond*, Vertical Editions, Skipton, 2004

Toshack, John, *Tosh: An Autobiography*, Arthur Barker Ltd, London, 1982

Various, *Farewell Ninian Park*, Media Wales, Cardiff, 2009

Yassine, Ali, *Was it Something I said? The voice of Cardiff City*, Y Lolfa, Ceredigion, 2011

In addition to these works, we have been grateful to old copies of the *South Wales Echo*, *Football Echo* and *Western Mail*, two attics full of Cardiff City programmes and numerous back copies of the excellent Welsh international football magazine *The Dragon Has Landed*.

Amazingly, some useful information was even gleaned from our collection of a certain Cardiff City fanzine from days gone by. We will let you guess the title of that one though . . . we think we have given you enough answers already.

David & Gareth

Also from The History Press

The Worst Football Kits of All Time

Dave Moor

978-0-7524-5904-2

In the mad, money-driven world of football, some rather interesting and sometimes shocking kits have been worn upon the field of play. This book is a full-colour celebration of some of the most outrageous strips foisted upon the poor players and the loyal fans, from clashing colours and disastrous designs to surprising sponsors and bad luck omens. With some classics and some surprises too, *The Worst Football Kits of All Time* is set to delight fans young and old, from strips donned by Victorian gentleman to modern-day prima donnas. So which really is the worst? You decide…

Visit our website and discover thousands of other History Press books.

www.thehistorypress.co.uk